G000021655

CYCLING
around
LEICESTERSHIRE
& RUTLAND

COMPILED BY ARNOLD ROBINSON

Walk & Write Ltd
2000

Cycling around Series

© Arnold Robinson.

All rights reserved. 2000.

ISBN 1 874754 40 3

WALK & WRITE LTD.,
UNIT 1, MOLYNEUX BUSINESS PARK,
WHITWORTH ROAD,
DARLEY DALE, MATLOCK,
DERBYSHIRE.
DE4 2HJ
TEL/FAX 01629 - 735911

Printed, bound, marketed and distributed by Walk & Write Ltd.

© Text, - Arnold Robinson 1999
© Maps and photographs - Arnold Robinson 1999

First Published   - July 1995
This reprint - July 2000

ISBN 1 874754 40 3

British Library Cataloguing-in-Publication Data.
A catalogue record for this book is available from the British Library.

Please note - The maps in this guide are purely illustrative. You are encouraged to use the appropriate 1:50,000 O.S. map.

Meticulous research has been undertaken to ensure that this publication is highly accurate at the time of going to press. The publishers, however, cannot be held responsible for alterations, errors or omissions, but they would welcome notification of such for future editions.

Typeset in AGaramond - bold, italic and plain 10pt, 14pt and 18pt.

Printed by - Walk & Write Ltd
Designed and typset by Walk & Write Ltd.

Cover photograph - by Arnold Robinson
Cover design© Walk and Write Ltd. 2000.

The author on one of his rides exploring forest backways.

ABOUT THE AUTHOR

Arnold Robinson has been a dedicated cyclist for sixty years. In that time, he has cycled in every county in England and Wales, each region of Scotland, in Ireland and Europe. He first cycled around Leicestershire and Rutland in the thirties and has returned on many occasions to explore the cycling byways, its towns and especially its villages.

After spending most of his childhood in Derbyshire and Nottinghamshire, in 1939 he moved to Sheffield to join the Police Force. When he retired in 1969, he held the rank of Detective Chief Superintendent and was head of the Criminal Investigation Department of Sheffield and Rotherham. After a spell as Police Consultant to Yorkshire Television and in industrial security, he became a freelance writer, broadcaster and photographer on outdoor activities but mainly cycling.

He regularly contributes articles and photographs to cycling magazines and is the author of a series of regional cycling guides covering the whole of Britain. He was also a major contributor of routes for *'Cyclists' Britain'* published in 1985 by Ordnance Survey/Pan Books.

His first of nearly two hundred broadcasts on cycling was made ln 1939. For five years he was the presenter of BBC Radio Sheffield's cycling programme *'On your Bike'*.

CYCLING ROUTES AROUND LEICESTERSHIRE and RUTLAND

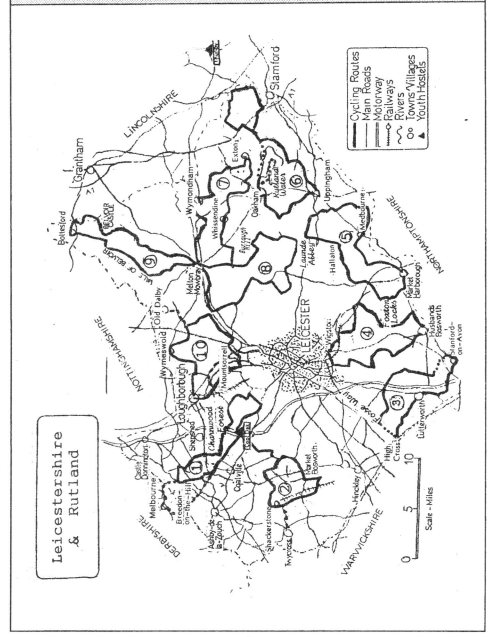

CONTENTS

Page No.

Key to ROUTE MAPS;

Cycling Routes.

Alternative Cycling Routes.

Main Roads.

Other Roads.

Unsurfaced roads and tracks.

Railways.

Rivers/Streams.

Lakes/Reservoirs.

Built up areas.

Towns/Villages.

Church.

Youth Hostel.

Camp Site.

Places of interest.

Summit.

Viewpoint.

KEY TO ABBREVIATIONS in ITINERARIES:

Inf: Tourist Information Office.
EC   Early Closing Day.
MD   Market Day.
BR: British Railway Passenger Station.
B&B   Bed & Breakfast accomodation.
YH   Youth Hostel.
Cafe   Cafe or Restaurant.
PM   Pub Meals.
Sh   Shops supplying food.
T: Toilets.
Cmg: Camp Sites.
Cvg: Caravan sites.
Sp: Signpost.
TR: Traffic island.
TL: Traffic lights.

An introduction to
CYCLING around
LEICESTERSHIRE and RUTLAND

Cyclists who reside in the City of Leicester are very fortunate. In whichever direction they ride, within a few miles they can be in quiet rural countryside and can follow byways which meander through woodlands and open fields. There is no extensive industrial belt as in many metropolitan areas. The few towns are relatively small and compact. To pass through them does not involve riding for mile after mile through a built up area.

It is true there are no mountains. The highest hills - Bardon Hill and Beacon Hill are less than 1,000 feet altitude although they appear higher when viewed from the surrounding countryside.

My first visit to the Hunting Shire was in June 1935 on a CTC Section ride to Belvoir. The following year we spent an Easter weekend in Charnwood Forest, still one of my favourite parts of the county. We were back again in October 1937 on a weekend at Bardon Hill Youth Hostel, long since closed. On another long weekend we explored the lovely byways and villages of Rutland.

For this guide, I have selected my favourite rides which present the county's many different faces; its most attractive villages and byways and places of interest.

The Routes.

The routes have been designed, so far as practicable, to follow quiet byways so avoiding the heavy traffic which bedevils the main roads on summer weekends and during holiday periods. By keeping to the byways, it is possible to ride for long periods seeing few motor vehicles.

Each of the rides could form the basis for a "day ride' or be combined into an on going tour. The rides could be commenced or finished at any point around the circuit eg. Ride No. 6 from Oakham might just as conveniently be commenced at Uppingham.

Some of the rides have optional extensions or diversions (see Notes at the foot of the itineraries). Alternatively, the mileage might be reduced by using one or more of the alternative routes indicated on the maps. Few of the rides involve strenuous hill climbs and on many of the routes it will be possible to ride all day without the need to dismount. Experienced riders might be able to cover two of the routes in one day.

Cyclists who are adept at planning their own routes will find the touring information useful when looking for a 'new' route or a variation of past tours.

The Towns.

Cyclists invariably try to avoid busy towns when planning their routes but apart from the City of Leicester itself, none of the towns in the county presents a serious problem to cycling. Some of the towns - Loughborough, Market Harborough, Ashby-de-la-Zouch and Uppingham now have ring roads or bypasses which take the through traffic away from the town centre's allowing cycling in traffic free conditions. Even the villages of Quorndon and Mountsorrell; Asfordby, Syston, Coalville, Measham, Great Glen and Billesdon are now bypassed all of which helps when looking for a quiet cycling route. For Touring information and other details of the various towns visited on the Rides see the Route itineraries.

The Villages.

The rides have been planned to allow visits to the most picturesque and interesting villages in the county (see Route itineraries) and time should be allowed to explore these. Well worth visiting are Newton Linford (Ride No 1) Market Bosworth (Ride No.2) Stanford-upon-Avon) (Ride No.3), Gumley (Ride No.4), Hallaton and Melbourne (Ride No.5); Edith Weston and Ryhall (Ride No 6); Edmondthorpe, Market Overton and Exton (Ride No 7); Loddington (Ride No 8); Goadby Marwood, Knipton and Woolsthorpe (Ride No 9) and Old Dalby (Ride No.10)

Places of Interest.

The rides also allow for visits to places of interest, castles, abbeys churches, historical sites and steam railways eg.
Bradgate Hall, Mount St. Bernard's Abbey and Breedon-on-the-Hill. (Ride No.1;
Bosworth Battlefield and Shackerstone Railway Centre (Ride No.2.); Stanford Hall and Church, and the Fosse Way (Ride No.3)
Grand Union Canal and Wistow (Ride No.4)
Foxton Locks, Hallaton and Medbourne (Ride No.5)
Uppingham, Wing Maze and Rutland Water (Ride No.6)
Stapleford Hall and Wymondham (Ride No.7)
Burrough-on-the-Hill and Country Park, and Frisby-on-the-Wreake (Ride No.8)
Vale of Belvoir and Belvoir Castle, Bottesford (Ride No.9)
Wymeswold and Mountsorrell (Ride No.10)

Accommodation.

The Department of Planning and Transport of the Leicestershire County Council produces annually an excellent Visitor's Guide which gives details of overnight accommodation in towns and villages throughout the county. (See Route Itineraries for locations) Details of accommodation may also be obtained from the various Tourist Information offices (See below) The CTC Handbook also contains details of recommended Bed & Breakfast accommodation.

The only Youth Hostel in the county is at Copt Oak on the edge of Charnwood Forest but there is also a hostel at Thurlby a few miles over the Lincolnshire border. (See page 48).

Camp Sites.

The location of Camp Sites is shown in the information Section of the Route Itineraries.

Tourist Information.

There are Tourist Information Offices at Leicester, Ashby-de-la-Zouch, Coalville, Hinckley, Loughborough, Market Bosworth, Market Harborough, Melton Mowbray, Oakham, and at Rutland Water.

Where to Eat.

The location of Cafes and pubs providing meals are shown in the itineraries but on routes through the more remote areas, it is advisable to carry emergency supplies of food and drink. The location of picnic sites is also shown.

Cycle Repairers.

Approved cycle repairers who carry a stock of spares and accessories and can also carry out emergency repairs are available in Leicester, Loughborough, Market Harborough, Oakham and at the Cycle Hire Centres at Rutland Water.

Maps.

The route maps are sufficiently detailed within the scope of the scale to enable the itinerary to be followed without difficulty but greater detail will be found on the Ordnance Survey Landranger Sheets Nos. 128, 129, 130, 140 and 141.

Other Publications.

The Leicestershire County Council have produced an attractive brochure giving details of five cycling routes which, when linked together, form a circuit tour of the county; also a set of three brochures 'Cycling around Rutland'. These are useful additions to the routes given in this guide.

CIRCULAR RIDE from COPT OAK YOUTH HOSTEL: CHARNWOOD FOREST and BREEDON - 30 MILES

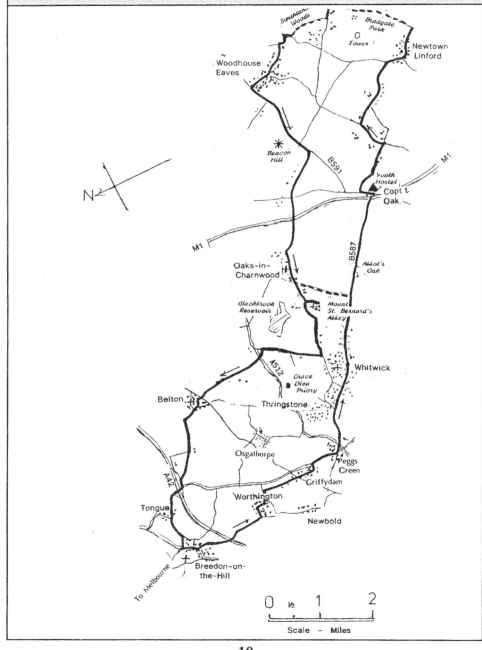

Scale - Miles

RIDE NO. 1
CIRCULAR RIDE from COPT OAK YOUTH HOSTEL ; CHARNWOOD FOREST and BREEDON. - 30.0 miles.

The ride starts from Copt Oak Youth Hostel and first makes a circuit of the best of Charnwood Forest visiting Bradgate Park, Swithland Woods and Mount St. Bernard's Abbey before heading westwards to Breedon-on-the-Hill with its prominent hilltop church. For cyclists wanting shorter rides, the ride might be divided into two parts; first by returning direct from Mount St. Bernard's Abbey to Copt Oak (17.5 miles); and on a future occasion starting the remainder of the route by riding direct to Belton (25.5 miles). There are also optional extensions of the route to include Melbourne and Calke Abbey both in Derbyshire and Staunton Harold. Additional distance: 8.0 miles.

Gradients: For the most part the gradients are gently undulating but there are a few climbs, eg. from Woodhouse Eaves to Beacon Hill, and around Breedon-on-the-Hill and on the extension to Melbourne, Calke Abbey and Staunton Harold.

Miles.	Places and route itinerary.	Information and Points of Interest.
	COPT OAK, From X rds alongside YH, take B591; N; take first turn R on byroad; in 1m at X rds turn L; desc and turn R (opp. entrance to Priory); cont to T junc; turn R into:	YH, for details see page 52. Cmg. Quiet byroad. Ruins of Ulverscroft Priory on L. Picturesque woods.
4.5	**NEWTON LINFORD.** Cont through village and turn L through gate into;	EC: Wed. B&B.Cafe. Attractive village and picturesque cottages.

Miles.	Places and route itinerary.	Information and Points of Interest.
1.0	**BRADGATE PARK.** Cont through park to exit gate; turn L on byroad and in half-mile, turn R on track through;	Deer Park. Surfaced drive. good cycling. Ruins of 16 cent. Bradgate House, birthplace of Lady Jane Grey. Tower on hillside "Old John" 1786
2.0	**SWITHLAND WOODS,** Cont through woods to exit; turn R on byroad; desc and keep to L at two junctions; climb to:	Slate Quarry Unsurfaced drive but all rideable. Woods especially attractive in spring and autumn.
1.5	**WOODHOUSE EAVES,** Cont through village to T junc; turn L (B591) and climb to summit near;	Sh. C. Pleasant village on lower slopes of Beacon Hill. Rocky scenery. Slate quarries. Country Park on L.
1.5	**BEACON HILL,** Desc to X rds and cont str ahead then take next turn R on byroad; at X rds cont str ahead, pass under bridge then turn L through:	Alt. 248m. second highest point in Leicestershire. Site of bronze age hill fort. Short walk to summit. Extensive views. M1 motorway.
3.0	**OAKS-IN-CHARNWOOD,** At X rds cont str ahead and in half-mile turn L into drive to:	B&B. Small village of scattered farms now spoiled by being so close to motorway although the noise is soon left behind.
1.0	**MOUNT ST. BERNARDS ABBEY,** Return to entrance, turn L and take next turn R; desc and in one-mile fork L to X rds (junc A512); cont str ahead to X rds (junc B5324); cont str ahead into:	Visit to abbey church recommended. Calvary. Impressive setting. Care when crossing A 512.
3.0	**BELTON,** Cont past church and turn R; cont through open country and at T junc; turn L to TR; turn R over bridge (A42) and in half-mile, turn L to:	Small unspectacular village. Quiet little used byroad.

Miles	Places and route itinerary.	Information and Points of Interest.
2.5	**TONGUE,** Cont through the village and turn R into;	Small isolated village.
1.0	**BREEDON-on-the-HILL,** Turn L through village (see note a) and turn L on byroad; cross bridge (A42) climb to;	Saxon church on hilltop. Strenuous climb but worth while for extensive views. Limestone cliffs of quarry. Lock-up in village. See note a
1.5	**WORTHINGTON,** At X rds turn L then R; turn L and take next turn R on narrow byroad; cont to X rds (B5324) at:	Small village through which lanes weave their way.
1.5	**GRIFFYDAM,** Cont str ahead; at junc A447 turn R and in half-mile at X rds at:	Straggling hamlet alongside the A447.
0.5	**PEGGS GREEN,** Turn L (B587); at next X rds cont str ahead to:	A complex junction where the A512 from Loughborough crosses the A447, but the route keeps to B roads.
2.0	**WHITWICK,** Cont ahead climbing along ridge road and cross motorway bridge to:	A large village on W edge of Charnwood Forest. Church has prominent tower.
3.5	**COPT OAK.**	

NOTE.
(a)   To extend the ride to include MELBOURNE and CALKE ABBEY (both in Derbyshire) and/or STAUNTON HAROLD, take the byroad from BREEDON-on-the-HILL to Wilson and MELBOURNE (Hall, Pool, Sh. C.); then climb to TICKNALL where turn L into CALKE PARK and to ABBEY (NT). Cont past church and leave Park; turn R through Calke Village then turn L; desc. then climb to junc.A453; turn R and then turn R into drive to STAUNTON HAROLD (Hall, C. Church NT). Return to A453 and turn R; at X rds cont str ahead (B587) and join the above route at PEGGS GREEN. Additional mileage 7.

CIRCULAR RIDE from COPT OAK Youth Hostel: MARKET BOSWORTH and BOSWORTH FIELD - 33 MILES

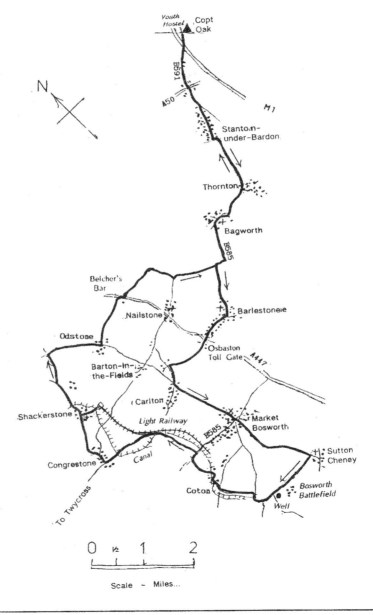

Scale – Miles...

RIDE NO. 2
CIRCULAR RIDE from COPT OAK Youth Hostel; MARKET BOSWORTH and BOSWORTH FIELD.
- 33.0 miles

To the south west of Copt Oak is an area of rural countryside less spectacular than the scenery in Charnwood Forest but there is a network of quiet byroads excellent for leisurely cycling. The main centre of the area is Market Bosworth and nearby is the site of the Battle of Bosworth Field where Richard III was killed. At Shackerstone, there is a railway centre and near to the route is Twycross Zoo, home of the chimpanzees in the tea advertisements featured on TV.

Gradients:
There are few hills of any consequence on this ride; the route is gently undulating throughout..

Miles.	Places and route itinerary.	Information and Points of Interest.
	COPT OAK. From X RDS, Take B591 SW; cross motorway bridge and At TR (junc A50), cont str ahead; in half-mile fork R into:	YH for details see page 52
2.0	**STANTON-under-BARDON.** Cont through village and at T junc. turn L on byroad; at outskirts of:	Straggling village on S slopes of Charnwood Forest. B&B at Markfield in E.
1.5	**THORNTON (junction).** Turn R and climb to;	
1.0	**BAGWORTH.** Join B585; cont to T junc; turn R then L to:	Hilltop village.
2.5	**BARLESTONE.** In centre of village, turn R (B582) to X rds at:	

Miles.	Places and route itinerary.	Information and Points of Interest.
1.0	**OSBASTON TOLL GATE.** Cont str ahead and at X rds, turn L to outskirts of;	Cross roads on A447 Hinckley to Ibstock road. Care when crossing.
1.5	**CARLTON,** Turn L to:	
2.0	**MARKET BOSWORTH,** From Market Place, take narrow field road through open country to outskirts of:	B&B. SH. C. Cmg. Attractive old town; Market Place 18/19 cent. house. Assoc with Dr. Samuel Johnson who taught at the school. Church - 14 cent. font, ancient chest.
2.5	**SUTTON CHENEY.** Turn R to:	B&B.
1.0	**BOSWORTH BATTLEFIELD,** Entrance to Country Park on L. On leaving turn L; at T junc turn R then take second L on narrow byroad; at T junc near canal bridge, turn R and imm turn L through:	Battlefield Exhibition Centre. C. T. Pic-nic site. Open: March-Oct. Well at which Richard III drank in 1485 shortly before he was killed in battle.
2.0	**COTON,** Cross canal and at T junc turn R then L; again cross canal and imm turn L; again cross canal; turn R into:	Farming hamlet Ashby-de-la-Zouch ca-nal. Quiet country byroad.
3.0	**CONGRESTONE.** (See note a) Fork L past church and then turn R to:	B&B. Unspectacular but pleasant village.
1.0	**SHACKERSTONE.** Turn R (cul-de-sac) and cross canal to RAILWAY CENTRE; retrace route to centre of village and turn R; cross canal and in half-mile fork R; at X rds. turn R to:	Quiet village. Preserved railway station.

Miles	Places and route itinerary.	Information and Points of Interest.
3.0	**ODSTONE.** Turn L to:	Farming Village.
1.0	**BELCHER'S BAR.** At T junc (A447) turn R; imm turn L; cont to T junc and turn L then fork R; in 1m turn L (B585) rejoining out- ward route; cont into:	Road junc. on A447. B&B - 1m S at Nailstone. Quiet byroads through open country.
3.5	**BAGWORTH.** Cont through village and imm after church, turn L; cont to:	Retrace outward route.
1.0	**THORNTON (Junc).** Turn L and climb for 1m then turn R and climb through:	
1.5	**STANTON-under-BARDON ,** Cont ahead and at T junc. turn L; at TR (junc A50), cont ahead and climb to:	See above.
2.0	**COPT OAK.**	

NOTE
(a). For TWYCROSS and ZOO; From junc at approach to CONGRESTONE, continue
straight ahead through Bilstone to TWYFORD. Return same route to CONGRESTONE.
The Zoo is along the A453 Ashby-de-la-Zouch road and is open daily: 7 miles return from
CONGRESTONE.

CIRCULAR RIDE from LUTTERWORTH:
STANFORD-ON-AVON and HIGH CROSS - 28.5 MILES

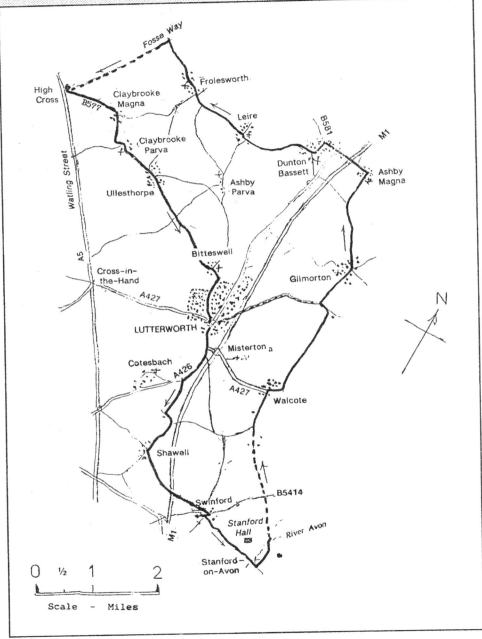

RIDE NO. 3
CIRCULAR RIDE from LUTTERWORTH;
Stanford-on-Avon and High Cross.
- 28.5 miles.

The main centre in the southern tip of the county is Lutterworth, an ancient town on rising ground above the River Swift. Nearby traffic on the A1 rushes north and south leaving Lutterworth quiet and perhaps more like it was in the days when stage coaches called on their long journey to London. This route first turns south to Stanford-on-Avon part of which is across the border in Northhamptonshire. After a short off-highway route, a byroad then runs through a succession of villages finally following an unsurfaced section of the Fosse Way to High Cross at the junction with Watling Street. The ride may be divided into two by turning left between Walcote and Gilmorton and riding direct to LUTTERWORTH.

Gradients: Very easy riding throughout with no hills to justify dismounting.

Miles.	Places and route itinerary.	Information and Points of Interest.
	LUTTERWORTH. From town centre, turn S on A426; cross bridge and at TL (junc of A427); cont ahead; in 1m turn L on byroad to:	EC: Wed; MD: Thurs. Sh. C. River Swift. Church: assoc. with John Wycliffe who was vicar for 19 years. Old coaching town.
3.0	**SHAWELL.** At X rds turn L to:	Assoc. with Lord Tennyson who visited the rectory.
2.0	**SWINFORD,** At junc B5414, turn R and then L on byroad to...	Small pleasant village.
1.5	**STANFORD-on-AVON.** Cross bridge and at church turn L; cross bridge and in 200 yds turn L through gate; follow field road and at junc (B5414) cont str ahead on field road; at T junc turn R on byroad and cont to:	River Avon, here little more than a stream, is the county boundary with Northants. The Hall (NT) is in Leicestershire but the church is in Northants. Monument in field to Pilcher, aviation pioneer who was killed here.

19

Miles.	Places and route itinerary.	Information and Points of Interest.
3.5	**WALCOTE.** At T junc. (A427) turn R and in 300 yds turn L on byroad; at T junc turn L then R into:	
3.0	**GILMORTON.** Turn L through village then turn R; in 1.5 miles fork L; cross bridge (M1) and at X rds (junc A426) cont str ahead to:	Quiet byroads ideal for leisurely cycling. Care when crossing A426.
2.5	**DUNTON BASSETT.** In centre of village turn L to:	B&B.
1.5	**LEIRE.** Cont str ahead to:	SC.
1.5	**FROLESWORTH.** Cont through village and in 1m at X rds. turn L; cont on unsurfaced field road (gated) to:	Route now follows Fosse Way, a Roman Road.
3.0	**HIGH CROSS.** Turn L (B577) to:	Junction of Fosse Way and Watling Street. Cross Former Roman Station of Venonae.
1.0	**CLAYBROOK MAGNA.** Cont through:	First of several small villages strung along the B577 road to LUTTERWORTH.
1.0	**CLAYBROOK PARVA.** Cont ahead through:	
1.0	**ULLESTHORPE.** Cont through:	
2.5	**BITTESWELL.** Into:	Small village now almost linked to LUTTERWORTH.
1.5	**LUTTERWORTH.**	

The Hall of the lovely village of GUMLEY visited on Ride No. 4 has been demolished but the fine clock tower still rises above the cottages.

SOUTH OF LEICESTER - 32.5 MILES

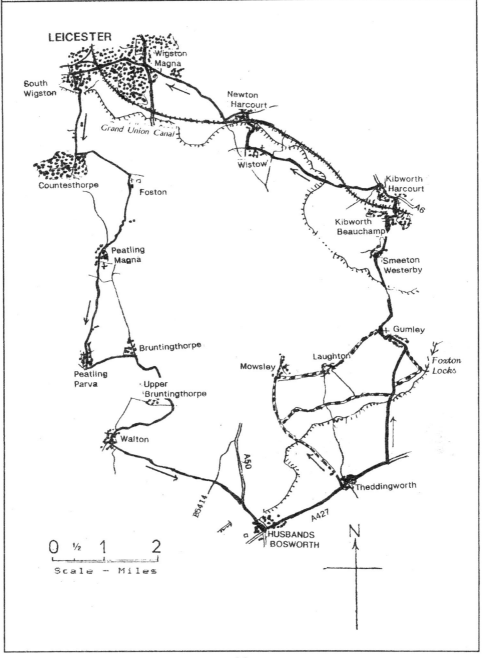

LEICESTER

Wigston Magna

South Wigston

Newton Harcourt

Grand Union Canal

Wistow

Kibworth Harcourt

A6

Countesthorpe

Foston

Kibworth Beauchamp

Peatling Magna

Smeeton Westerby

Gumley

Bruntingthorpe

Laughton

Foxton Locks

Peatling Parva

Mowsley

Upper Bruntingthorpe

Walton

A50

Theddingworth

B5414

A427

HUSBANDS BOSWORTH

N

0   ½   1   2

Scale - Miles

RIDE NO. 4

SOUTH OF LEICESTER.
- 32.5 miles.

This ride is ideal for cyclists resident in the south of the city of LEICESTER. The route starts from South Wigston which is now a busy suburb but this is quickly left behind as quiet traffic free byroads are followed through a delightful rural area. Although there are no highlights, the route passes through some secluded countryside and pleasant villages.

Only occasionally does it involve riding along a main road.

Gradients: Most of this ride is gently undulating the only hills of any consequence being a short climb after leaving Walton and another on the A427 into Husbands Bosworth. There is a short climb into Gumley and another into Smeeton Westerby.

Miles.	Places and route itinerary.	Information and Points of Interest.
	SOUTH WIGSTON. Leave by Countesthorpe Road; turn left then bear right; cross canal and continue to outskirts of:	Sh. Busy suburb of Leicester. Cyc. Car Park on Countesthorpe Road. Grand Union Canal.
2.0	**COUNTESTHORPE.** Turn left (sp Foston Church) and in one-mile turn R to:	Former village enlarged in recent years.
1.0	**FOSTON.** Continue on narrow field road and at T junc turn left into:	Site of medieval village St. Bartholemew's church; 10 cent. Memorial to Faunt's.
1.5	**PEATLING MAGNA.** Continue ahead to:	Small pleasant village.
2.0	**PEATLING PARVA.** At T junc turn left and at second T junc. again turn left to outskirts of:	Quiet village.
1.0	**BRUNTINGTHORPE.** At T junc turn right away from centre of village; in 3 miles turn left through:	

Miles.	Places and route itinerary.	Information and Points of Interest.
3.0	**WALTON.** Turn left on byroad and in half-mile fork left; after short climb descend to X rds (B5414); continue straight ahead; in further half-mile at T junction (A427) turn right; climb; (one way system) into:	Small village in open countryside with extensive view. Thatched cottages.
3.5	**HUSBANDS BOSWORTH.** Turn left (A427) in village and continue to:	EC: Wed & Thurs. Church has 14 cent. tower. Village green. Georgian Hall.
2.0	**THEDDINGWORTH.** (see note a) Continue through village and in one-mile, turn left on byroad; in one-mile cross canal and climb to X rds; continue str ahead, (sp Gumley); (see note b).Descend then climb to T junc; turn L and climb through:	EC: Thurs. Church in picturesque location. Source of River Welland.
5.0	**GUMLEY.** Continue through village and turn right; descend and cross canal bridge and climb into:	One of the most picturesque villages in Leicestershire. Views. PM. 19 cent. cottages. Ancient village. recorded in Domesday Book. Hall built in 1764 was demolished in 1964 but clock tower remains.
2.0	**SMEETON WESTERBY.** Turn right thrugh village and continue to:	Picturesque cottages.
1.0	**KIBWORTH BEAUCHAMP.** At T junc turn right then left then continue to:	EC: Thurs. Sh. Church has a restored screen. Pleasant cottages.
0.5	**KIBWORTH HARCOURT.** Turn L (A6) and in half-mile turn left on byroad; continue to:	EC: Thurs. Sh. Large village on A6, once the main road from London to Manchester. Old houses. Grammar School. 1725.

Miles	Places and route itinerary.	Information and Points of Interest.
3.0	**WISTOW.** Immediately after cattle grid turn Right on narrow byroad; cross canal and railway bridges and continue into:	Cafe in garden centre on left.
1.0	**NEWPORT HARCOURT.** At T junc. turn left and at next T junc. turn R continue to:	Pleasant village. Elizabethan Manor House where King Charles II slept after the Battle of Naseby.
2.5	**WIGSTON PARVA.** At X rds (TL) continue straight ahead to:	EC: Wed. Former Village is now an outer suburb of Leicester. Has two churches; All Saints and St. Woolstan's.
1.5	**SOUTH WIGSTON.**	

NOTES.

(a) From THEDDINGWORTH, there are several alternative byway routes to GUMLEY (See map) Scenically there is little to choose between the alternatives, the distance is approximately the same.

(b) A short distance beyond the cross roads, a field road on the right leads in half-mile to FOXTON LOCKS (see Ride No.5)

On Ride No. 4 byroads lead to the peaceful village of Smeeton Westerby which has some picturesque cottages.

25

CIRCULAR RIDE around MARKET HARBOROUGH:
Foxton Locks, Loddington & Medbourne. - 43 MILES

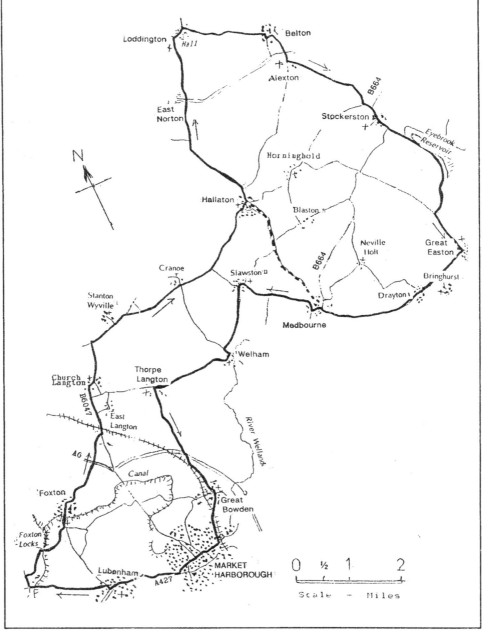

RIDE NO. 5
CIRCULAR RIDE around MARKET HARBOROUGH;
Foxton Locks, Loddington & Medbourne.
- 43.0 miles.

Market Harborough sits astride the infant River Welland in the south east corner of the county. It is a small but bustling place which has been bypassed in recent years. Before starting the ride it is worth seeing the picturesque Grammar School and the nearby church which has a fine spire. The first objective along the ride is the 'staircase' of canal locks at Foxton. The ride then continues along quiet country byways passing through sleepy villages. We next head for Hallaton, a quiet corner with a market cross and an imposing church, and then to Loddington, another attractive village. From Hallaton, the ride may be shortened by riding direct to Medbourne whose packhorse bridge and church make a delightful picture.

Gradients.

Undulating with some very easy riding for the first few miles. There are some hilly sections on the optional extension after Hallaton. The return from Medbourne is easy.

Miles.	Places and route itinerary.	Information and Points of Interest.
	MARKET HARBOROUGH. Leave by A427 W and cont to:	EC: Thurs; MD: Tues. BR. Sh. C. B&B. SC. River Welland. Church; spire. Large Market square. Timbered houses on pillars. c.1614. "Three Swans' inn sign.
2.0	**LUBENHAM.** Turn R on byroad and imm. fork L; cont through open country and cross canal; at X rds turn R and then again turn R; cont to:	EC: Thurs. Sh, SC.

Miles.	Places and route itinerary.	Information and Points of Interest.
2.5	**FOXTON LOCKS.** cross canal bridge and in half-mile turn L and cross canal into:	Access along track at side of Grand Union canal. Staircase of ten locks which lift canal 75ft. built in 1808 and now used solely by pleasure craft.
1.0	**FOXTON Village.** Cont through village and in one-mile at X rds, cont str ahead and at T junc (B6047) turn L to:	B&B. C. Attractive village Manor House. Church; 13 cent. Cross.
3.0	**CHURCH LANGTON.** Turn R past church and cont to T junc; turn R passing lane on L into:	Beautiful village. Centre of group of Langton villages. Church: impressive tower. Rectory.
1.5	**STANTON WYVILLE.** Take next turn R and cont through;	Hamlet in cul-de-sac.
1.5	**CRANOE.** Cont ahead to:	Small village with little of interest.
2.5	**HALLATON.** (See note a) Turn L in village and in half-mile fork L; climb for one mile then desc to X rds at:	B&B. SC. Sh, Unusual conical market cross, Imposing St, Michael's church. Annual custom of bottle kicking on Easter Monday. Castle Hill Camp - earthwork.
2.5	**EAST NORTON.** Cross A57 and cont str ahead; cross Eye Brook then climb; desc into:	Care when crossing A47.
1.5	**LODDINGTON.** Turn R in village then again turn R; cont on hilly byroad to:	Picturesque village. Quiet location. Impressive church.
2.0	**BELTON.** Turn L then R and cont to X rds (A47) at:	B&B. SC. Cmg. Care when crossing main road.
0.5	**ALLEXTON.** Cont ahead and in half-mile turn L (opp church) on narrow byroad; at T junc (B664), turn R through;	Pleasant byroad through Eye Brook valley.

Miles	Places and route itinerary.	Information and Points of Interest.
3.0	**STOCKERSTON.** When B664 turns R, cont str ahead alongside Eye Brook Reservoir then climb to T junc; turn L and desc to:	Eye Brook reservoir. Wild life.
3.5	**GREAT EASTON.** Turn R and cont to:	Pleasant village. Quiet byroads.
2.0	**DRAYTON.** Cont ahead to:	
4.5	**MEDBOURNE.** Turn R and then turn L at church; in 250 yds again turn L to:	B&B. Attractive village. Roman Road once passed through village. Ford. Packhorse bridge and church make a delightful picture.
2.0	**SLAWSTON.** Turn L then desc; at T junc turn L into:	Small isolated village.
1.5	**WELHAM.** Cont though village to:	River Welland is here the county boundary with Northants.
1.5	**THORPE LANGTON.** Turn L; cross bypass and cont into:	
2.5	**GREAT BOWDEN.** Cont str through village and at T junc (A427) turn R into:	River Welland. Now virtually a suburb of MARKET HARBOROUGH.
2.0	**MARKET HARBOROUGH.**	

NOTE:

(a) The ride may be shortened to 26.5 miles by turning R in HALLATON and riding direct to MEDBOURNE.

CIRCULAR RIDE from OAKHAM:
UPPINGHAM and RUTLAND WATER - 41 MILES

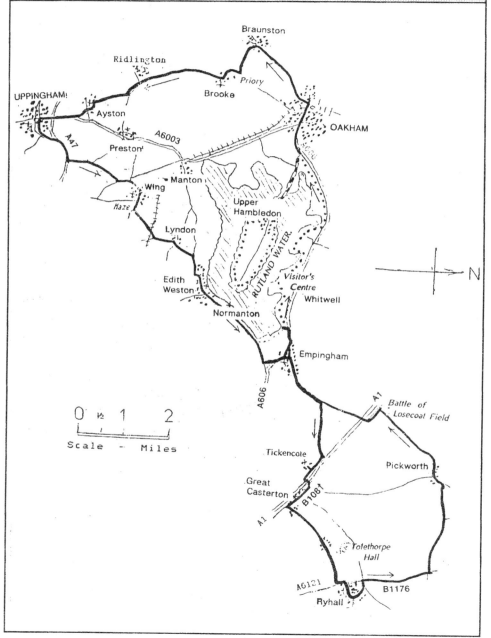

RIDE NO. 6
CIRCULAR RIDE from OAKHAM; UPPINGHAM and RUTLAND WATER.
- 41.0 miles.

The ride is confined to the byways of Rutland England's smallest county . Starting from the old world town of Oakham, it first follows byways through Braunston to Uppingham, another attractive old town which has an ancient public sschool. It then turns north to Wing where there is a turf maze. After the lovely village of Edith Weston, the route makes a circuit of Rutland Water, the largest man-made lake in the country. Since Dave Archer opened his Cycle Hire Centre here, cyclists have been attracted to the area. They are able to ride along a specially constructed cycle track which makes a circuit of the Reservoir (see brochure available at Cycle Hire Centre). The ride to Great Casterton and Ryhall on the border with Lincolnshire may be omitted. There are several vaiations of the route - see notes and map.

Gradients:
The early miles through Braunston to Uppingham and on to Rutland Water have some climbs although they are not too strenuous. It is then easier riding.

Miles.	Places and route itinerary.	Information and Points of Interest.
	OAKHAM. From town centre, take A606 and after level crossing turn L; then imm. turn L again; climb then cont to:	EC: Thurs.; MD: Wed.Sat. BR. B&B. Sh. C. Church: 12-15 cent. Grammar School. Butter Cross and Stocks. Castle 12 cent. Banquetting Hall has collection of horse shoes. Museum.
2.5	**BRAUNSTON.** Turn L then keep to L and cont to T junc; turn R to:	B&B. SC.
1.5	**BROOKE.** Cont ahead and climb to outskirts of:	Priory ruins, 17 cent. Church: box pews. River Gwash.

Miles.	Places and route itinerary.	Information and Points of Interest.
2.0	**RIDLINGTON.** See note a. Cont ahead and turn R to:	Church: collection of musical instruments.
1.5	**AYSTON.** Cont to T junc (A6003) turn R and at X rds cont str ahead into:	
1.0	**UPPINGHAM.** Turn L through town centre; at junc A47, turn R then turn L on byroad; cont to:	EC: Thurs. MD:Wed. B&B. Sh. C. Public School, 16 cent. Attractive old town.
3.0	**WING.** Cont through village then fork L; cont to:	B&B. Turf maze, 40ft. diam.
1.5	**LYNDON.** At entrance to village, turn R then imm. L on field road; at T junc. turn R then turn L into:	Village in woods in agricultural area. SC. Church.
1.5	**EDITH WESTON.** In half-mile at X rds, cont str ahead to:	B&B. SC. Pict village on south side of Rutland Water. Church.
1.0	**NORMANTON.** (See note b) Cont ahead and at X rds, turn L; at junc A606 turn L and climb to:	CH. Former Church on headland is now a Museum.
2.0	**EMPINGHAM.** (See note c). Turn R past church and at X rds again turn R; cont into open country and at X rds turn R to :	B&B. Church - paintings. Picturesque village streets.
3.0	**TICKENCOTE.** Cont ahead under bridge (A1) and cont into:	Small village lying aside of A1. Church: arch. bells.
1.0	**GREAT CASTERTON.** Cont through village and after church, turn L on byroad to:	On Ermine Street, former Roman Road, later Great North Road, now bypassed. Cmg. SC. Old inns and houses.

Miles	Places and route itinerary.	Information and Points of Interest.
1.5	**LITTLE CASTERTON.** Cont to T junc; turn L then turn R into:	
2.0	**RYHALL,** Turn L and at junc with A6121, turn L then turn R (B1176); at X rds turn L; in woods again turn L and in 1m, turn L into:	Pict. village. 'Green Dragon' Inn.
4.5	**PICKWORTH.** Cont ahead to T junc alongside A1; turn L and in half-mile turn R under bridge; cont on byroad; at X rds cont ahead retracing outward route and cont into:	Small village near to Clipsham Stone Quarries. Arch of ruined church. Site of Battle of Losecoat Field.
5.5	**EMPINGHAM.** Join A606 then turn L to SYKES LANE CAR PARK.: join Cycling Trail to:	See above.
2.0	**RUTLAND WATER.** From Visitors Centre, follow Cycle Trail westwards alongside Reservoir to :	Visitors Centre. C. CH. Most of Trail can be ridden.
1.5	**BARNSDALE CAR PARK.** Cont on Trail first alongside Reservoir and then turn L on special cycle track alongside A606; rejoin A606 (see note b) and cont into:	Picnic area.
2.5	**OAKHAM.**	

NOTES.

(a)　From Ridlington, there is a more direct route to WING via PRESTON but this omits UPPINGHAM.

(b)　From NORMANTON, there is a shorter way by turning L on to the Trail across the top of the Dam. This leads direct to the SYKES LANE CAR PARK.

(c)　The extension of the ride to GREAT CASTERTON AND RYHALL may be omitted by following the route across the Dam (see (b) above) and then turning L to the RUTLAND WATER VISITORS CENTRE, reducing the total mileage to 23.5.

(d)　The ride may be extended by turning L off the A606 on a byroad to the UPPER HAMBLEDEN peninsula and following the cycling trail, then returning to the A606. Distance : 7.5 miles return.

(e)　Full details of the RUTLAND WATER CYCLING CIRCUIT and the facilities are available in a brochure obtainable from the CYCLE HIRE CENTRE.

On Ride No. 9 there is a view of the towers of Belvoir Castle rising above the trees.

The church and packhorse bridge at the secluded village of Medbourne,
a highlight on Ride No. 5.

CIRCULAR RIDE from MELTON MOWBRAY: WYMONDHAM, EXTON and WHISSENDINE - 34 MILES

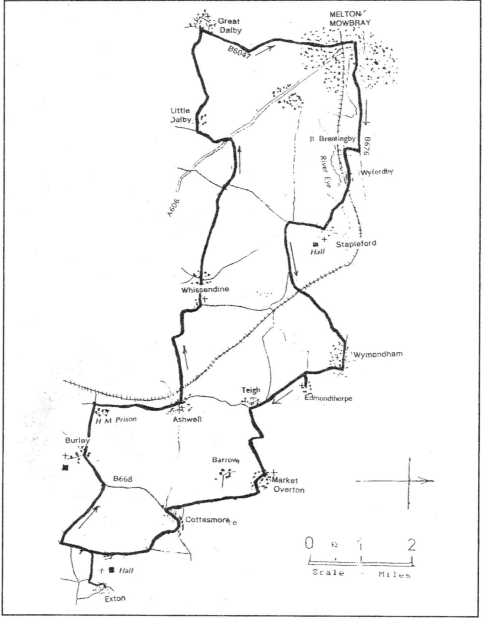

RIDE NO. 7
CIRCULAR RIDE from MELTON MOWBRAY: WYMONDHAM, EXTON and WHISSENDINE.
34.0 miles.

To the south east of MELTON MOWBRAY is a network of quiet byroads which criss-cross the Vale of Catmose. They provide some excellent cycling routes which link together some delightful and secluded villages. This ride might also be linked with Ride No.6 (see Note a) or could in fact be started from OAKHAM (see note b).

Gradients.

The gradients are very gentle, the altitude only varying from approx. 300 to 400 ft.

Miles.	Places and route itinerary.	Information and Points of Interest.
	MELTON MOWBRAY. From Town Centre, leave by Sherrard St. and Thorpe End then fork R along Saxby Road (B676); in 1.5 miles, turn R to :	See Ride No.8.
2.0	**BRENTINGBY.** Cont through :	Narrow byroad.
0.5	**WYFORDBY.** Cross level crossing then River Eye; cont to:	
1.0	**STAPLEFORD.** At T junc turn R then keep L at several juncs. cross level crossing and climb easily; at T junc turn R into:	Hall, impressive; church Road runs alongside extensive parkland.
4.0	**WYMONDHAM.** Cont along village street turn R on byroad and in one-mile, turn L to :	EC:Thurs; Church - tower. carving, effigy of knight; Stilton Cheese originated here. Ancient market town.

37

Miles.	Places and route itinerary.	Information and Points of Interest.
1.0	**EDMONDTHORPE.** Return to junc. and turn L; cont to:	Hall - Tudor. Ancient tree.
1.5	**TEIGH.** Turn L and climb to :	B&B, Church; pews, Prayer loft. Village pumps.
1.5	**MARKET OVERTON.** In centre of village, turn R; in one-mile pass byroad to :	Church; Saxon round tower, Prayer loft, arch, painting, sundial. Thatched Inn. Stocks, Whipping Post.
1.0	**BARROW.** Cont ahead and at T junc (B668) turn L into :	Thatched cottages. Cross.
1.5	**COTTESMORE.** When B668 turns sharply to L; turn R on byroad; at T junc turn R and in one-mile turn L; in half-mile again turn L into :	Gave name to famous Hunt and to nearby RAF Station. B&B. SC. Thatched cottages. St. Nicholas' Church. Road follows wall alongside Exton Park.
3.0	**EXTON.** Retrace route for one-mile and at T junc, turn L; in half-mile turn R; at T junc (B668) turn L to:	B&B. Picturesque thatched cottages built of local stone surround village green. Hall in ruins in parkland. Barnsdale Avenue, tree lined.
3.5	**BURLEY.** Turn R on byroad and in one-mile at X rds, turn R to:	B&B. Burley House. Ashwell Open Prison on R. Cottesmore Hunt kennels.
2.0	**ASHWELL.** In centre of village, turn L, and cont to:	Pleasant village, thatched cottages. Church. Well.
2.5	**WHISSENDINE.** Cont through village and in 3m at X rds (A606), cont str ahead; in 1m turn R to :	EC:Thurs. B&B. Church: windows, 14 cent tower. Windmill. Care when crossing busy road.
4.0	**LITTLE DALBY.** Cont ahead to :	

Miles	Places and route itinerary.	Information and Points of Interest.
2.0	**GREAT DALBY.** Turn R through village and cont on B6047 to:	See Ride No.8.
3.0	**MELTON MOWBRAY.**	

NOTES.

(a) Part of Ride No.6 a circuit of Rutland Water may be joined by riding from Exton to the RUTLAND WATER VISITORS CENTRE (see map) returning to this ride at ASHWELL.

(b) This ride might be started by riding from OAKHAM to ASHWELL, returning from EXTON (see map).

The church at Stanford-on-Avon is in a poor state but is has some interesting monuments. Ride No. 3.

CIRCULAR RIDE from MELTON MOWBRAY:
Burrough Hill and Launde Abbey - 41 MILES

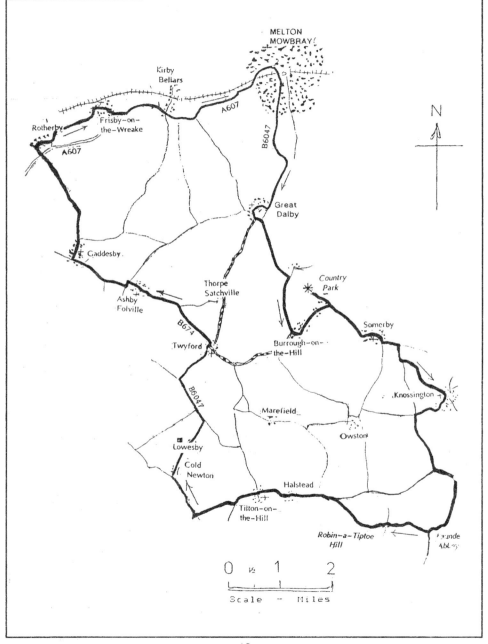

RIDE NO. 8
CIRCULAR RIDE from
MELTON MOWBRAY :
Burrough Hill & Launde Abbey.
- 41.0 miles.

The Leicestershire Wolds sprawl across the map to the south of Melton Mowbray in the triangle formed by the A607 road to Leicester on the west; the A606 Oakham road on the east and the A47 Leicester - Oakham road to the south. It is an area of unspoiled rolling countryside of woods and meadows only penetrated by two B roads which meet at Twyford before climbing to Tilton-on-the-Hill. It is exhilerating cycling countryside along usually deserted and occasionally gated byroads.

Gradients:
Whichever route is taken through this area, there are almost continual climbs and descents but the climbs are relatively short and do not present a serious problem.

Miles.	Places and route itinerary.	Information and Points of Interest.
	MELTON MOWBRAY. From Town Centre, leave by B6047 and continue through open country to:	EC:Thurs; MD:Tues. Sh. C. BR. B&B. Cmg. Famous for Stilton Cheese and Pork Pies. Church: St. Mary's. W porch and windows; tower. Sir Malcolm Sargent was organist and choirmaster here for ten years. Bede House, 17 cent. museum. Anne of Cleeves House. Fox Hunting Centre. River Eye.
3.0	**GREAT DALBY.** Cont through village and when the B6047 turns R; cont str ahead on byroad; climb for 1m to:	B&B. The road to Great Dalby crosses a war-time airfield. Royal Oak Inn. Pleasant village. Church - squat tower, west front.

Miles.	Places and route itinerary.	Information and Points of Interest.
3.0	**BURROUGH-on-the-HILL.** Turn L through village and climb for 1m; turn L to:	Small hilltop village, views. Post Office formerly a farmhouse. Manor House, Stone cottages. Church; 13 cent.
1.0	**BURROUGH HILL.** Retrace route and cont ahead to:	Country Park, picnic area, extensive views. Site of prehistoric hill fort.
1.5	**SOMERBY.** Turn L through village and at T junc turn R then L and cont to:	Pretty hilltop village Birthplace of two prominent surgeons; Cheseldon and Richardson.
2.0	**COLD OVERTON.** From centre of village, retrace route for 300 yds and turn L to:	Church - spire. Stone cottages.
2.0	**KNOSSINGTON.** At X rds, turn R into village and turn L past church, turn R on byroad and in half-mile turn L; cont through woods then turn L then R then desc steeply to:	Quiet hilltop village at hub of country byroads. Cmg. Lush meadows.
4.0	**LAUNDE.** Fork R and climb to X rds; cont str head and then bear L to:	Elizabethan House, few remians of Priory. Pict. location. River Chater. B&B.
3.0	**HALSTEAD.** Cont ahead and climb to:	Cross former railway line.
3.5	**TILTON-on-the-Hill.** At X rds cont str ahead (B6047) in half -mile turn R on byroad and at X rds turn R; desc steeply to:	Impressive church at X rds.
2.0	**COLD NEWTON.** Turn R to ;	Abandoned village. Manor House.
1.0	**LOWESBY.** Cont to T junc (B6047); turn L and cont to:	Hall - Georgian. Park. Queniborough Brook - flows westwards.

Miles	Places and route itinerary.	Information and Points of Interest.
2.5	**TWYFORD.** Turn L (B674) to:	Road junction.
2.0	**ASHBY FOLVILLE.** Cont ahead (B674) road junc at:	Model village. Church restored.
2.0	**GADDESBY.** Turn R through village and at first junc cont str ahead on byroad; at T junc (A607), cont str ahead into:	Picturesque. Church: impressive. South aisle. W doorway. Bench ends. Hall. Timber framed houses.
2.5	**ROTHERBY.** Turn R and at T junc turn L to:	
1.5	**FRISBY-on-the WREAKE.** Turn R through village and cont to T junc (A607); turn L and cont on main road through:	Sh. River Wreake. Village was previously on turnpike road. Interesting old houses. Wattle and Daub wall. Cross, 13 cent.
1.5	**KIRKBY BELLARS.** Cont ahead into:	Church: prominent spire.
3.0	**MELTON MOWBRAY.**	

NOTES;
(a) There are several variations of the route after Burrough-on-the Hill viz: (i) omitting Knossington, Launde, Cold Newton and Lowesby and riding direct to Twyford; (ii) Ashby Foville and Gaddesby, and/or (iii) Rotherby and Frisby-on-the-Wreake, and returning direct to MELTON MOWBRAY via Great Dalby, any of which will enable the distance to be reduced. (See map).

CIRCULAR RIDE from MELTON MOWBRAY:
VALE of BELVOIR and BOTTESFORD - 41.5 MILES

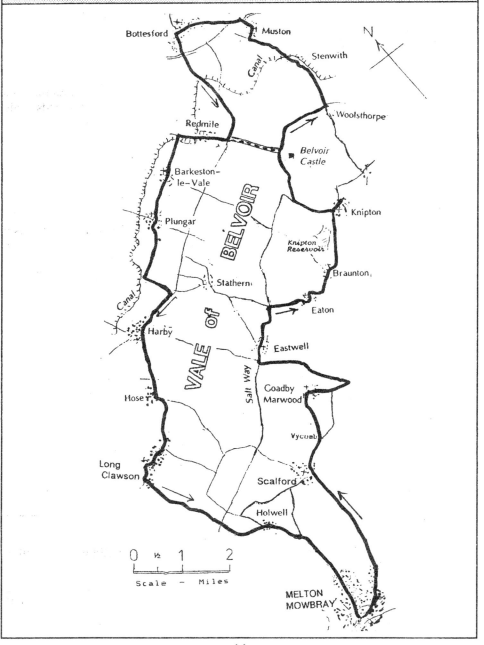

RIDE NO. 9
CIRCULAR RIDE fom MELTON MOWBRAY :
VALE of BELVOIR and BOTTESFORD.
- 41.5 miles.

This ride into the north of the county concentrates on the network of byways on either side of the Belvoir ridge. The highlight is the magnificent views of Belvoir Castle which crowns the northern end of a ridge of hills and looks down on the Vale. The ride from BELVOIR to BOTTESFORD involves crossing the county boundary into Lincolnshire for a few miles.

Gradients:
For the first five miles it is a steady climb until reaching the line of the Salt Way. It is then undulating without any major climbs. After Woolsthorpe, the ride is very easy until a final very steep climb from Long Clawson after which there is an easy descent back to Melton Mowbray.

Miles.	Places and route itinerary.	Information and Points of Interest.
	MELTON MOWBRAY. Leave town centre by Sherrard St. and Thorpe End; cont along Thorpe Rd and New Thorpe; in 1m turn L on byroad; climb steadily for 2 miles to outskirts of:	See Ride No.8.
4.0	**SCALFORD.** Do not turn into village but cont str ahead to:	Cottages nestle in hollow.
1.0	**WYCOMB.** Continue ahead and in half-mile at T junc, turn L; in further 1m turn L into:	Farming hamlet.
2.0	**GOADBY MARWOOD,** Retrace route and at T junc. in 1m turn sharp L; cont to X rds; turn R to:	B&B. Sc. Sleepy village. Church. Road now follows Salt Way.

Miles.	Places and route itinerary.	Information and Points of Interest.
4.0	**EASTWELL.** Turn R through village; and in half-mile at X rds turn R; desc through:	Church - stone screen.
2.0	**EATON.** After short climb cont to:	Pict. cottages on hillside.
1.0	**BRANSTON.** Turn L then R; cont to:	Pretty cottages and gardens.
1.5	**KNIPTON.** Retrace route and turn R; climb for half-mile then turn R through woods; desc to road junction at:	B&B. Pict. estate village. River Devon. Cross. Reservoir in wooded valley.
1.5	**BELVOIR.** (See note a) Turn R, cross county boundary and cont to X rds at:	C. T. Castle on ridge in beautiful situation. Seat of Dukes of Rutland, open to public. View of castle on R.
1.5	**WOOLSTHORPE.** Turn L through:	In Lincolnshire. Picturesque village.
1.0	**STENWITH.** Cont ahead, cross canal and then recross county boundary and turn R into:	Hamlet on former Grantham Canal abandoned 1936. Former Inn known as 'Dirty Duck'.
1.5	**MUSTON.** Cont to T junc (A52); turn L and at start of bypass turn R into:	Pleasant village. Direct byroad to BOTTESFORD closed due to construction of bypass but footpath available. Care when turning R.
1.5	**BOTTESFORD.** In centre of village turn L on by-road; in one-mile cross canal and cont to X rds; turn R to:	EC: Wed. Was formerly on A52 but is now bypassed and much quieter. Pict. corners. Whipping Post. Cross. Church: Rutland memorials.
3.5	**REDMILE.** Cross canal and in half-mile turn L and again cross canal; cont ahead through:	B&B. PM.

Miles	Places and route itinerary.	Information and Points of Interest.
1.5	**BARKESTON-in-the-Vale.** to:	B&B. Quiet farming village.
1.0	**PLUNGAR.** Cont ahead and at T junc turn R to outskirts of:	B&B. SC. Canal Wharf buildings (half-mile N).
3.0	**HARBY.** Turn L then R; cont through:	
1.5	**HOSE.** to:	
2.0	**LONG CLAWSON.** Cont through village and at T junc. turn L; climb for 1.5 miles to CLAWSON HILL; at X rds (Salt Way) cont str ahead and desc through:	B&B. Large village at foot of edge. Dairy has produced Stilton Cheese since 1911.
3.0	**HOLWELL.** Cont ahead and in one-mile turn R; and cont into:	B&B. Cmg. Former Ironstone mining in vicinity.
3.5	**MELTON MOWBRAY.**	

NOTE.

(a) The distance may be reduced by turning L at the BELVOIR junction and riding direct to REDMILE. Total distance then 32.0 miles.

CIRCULAR RIDE from LOUGHBOROUGH: WYMESWOLD and MOUNTSORRELL - 25.5.MILES

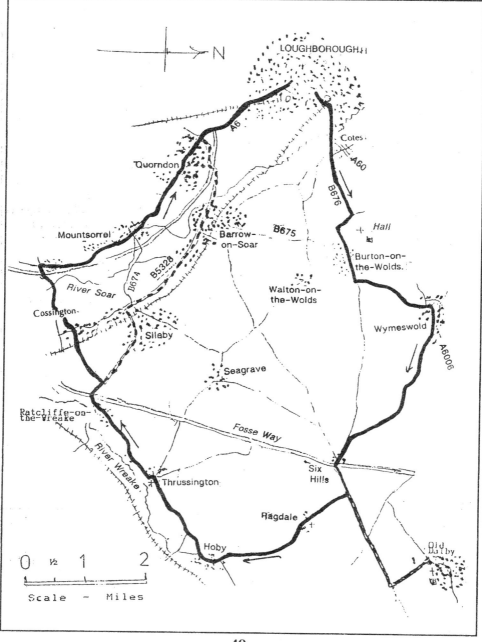

RIDE NO. 10
CIRCULAR RIDE
from LOUGHBOROUGH:
WYMESWOLD and
MOUNTSORRELL.
- 25.5 niles.

This ride starts by visiting some of the isolated villages on the Wolds to the east of LOUGHBOROUGH. The route then passes under the Fosse Way at Six Hills, which are not hills at all - it is merely the name of an ancient road junction - and then continues through open country before descending into the Wreake Valley. The return is through MOUNTSORRELL and QUORNDON, both of which are now bypassed by the A6 Loughborough - Leicester road. This means that cycling can be more enjoyable than was possible when the roads were heavily used by commercial vehicles. There is also an alternative route using B roads through SILEBY and BARROW-upon-SOAR.

Gradients: After crossing the River Soar at Cotes, there is a steady climb to WYMESWOLD, but after Six Hills, the gradients are very easy.

Miles.	Places and route itinerary.	Information and Points of Interest.
	LOUGHBOROUGH, Leave by Nottingham Road pass BR station; cont, on A60 and cross bridge (River Soar) to:	EC:Wed; MD;Mon, Thurs. BR. B&B, SC. C. Thriving industrial town. Bell foundry, est. 1858. Carillon Tower, 152 ft high. 47 bells. Steam Railway on former Great Central Rly. line.
2.0	**COTES,** When main road turns L, fork R (B676) and climb for one-mile; at T junc turn R then L and cont to climb into:	On the left is the Prestwold Estate. Church amongst trees in park.
3.0	**BURTON-on-the-WOLDS.** Cont through village and turn L on byroad to:	Noticeably extended in recent years. Hall.

Miles.	Places and route itinerary.	Information and Points of Interest.
2.0	**WYMESWOLD.** At T junc (A6006), turn R through village; turn R at church then turn L on byroad into open country; in 2m at T junc, turn L to:	An old Market town on cross-country road from Melton Mowbray to Hathern near to Nottinghamshire border. Church was restored in 1844.
3.0	**SIX HILLS.** Pass under bridge (A46 - Fosse Way); in half mile turn R (see note a) and desc. through:	An ancient road junction on Watling Street; once familiar to local cyclists but who now tend to avoid it.
1.5	**RAGDALE.** Cont ahead and desc to:	Church - picturesque, stone and brick tower. Old Hall.
2.0	**HOBY.** Cont through village and turn R to:	Small village in Wreake valley. Across the river and railway line is Brooksby. The Hall was once home of Admiral of the Fleet Lord Beatty of Battle of Rutland fame; is now an Agricultural College.
1.5	**THRUSSINGTON.** In centre of village, turn L then R and cont to:	
2.0	**RATCLIFFE-on-the WREAKE.** Turn R under bridge (A46) and then turn L on byroad; cont to:	Pass to west side of Fosse Way, Alternative ways from here. (See note b).
2.0	**COSSINGTON.** At X rds cont str ahead, cross bridge (River Soar) and at TR cont str ahead to X rds; turn R through:	Sh. Small village in Soar valley. Here the A6 new bypass is crossed.
3.0	**MOUNTSORREL.** Cont ahead through:	EC:Wed. B&B. Sh. River Soar. 18 cent. Market cross.
1.5	**QUORNDON (Quorn).** Cont ahead. join A6 at N end of bypass and cont into:	EC:Wed. B&B. Cmg. Gives its name to famous hunt. On northern edge of Charnwood Forest.
2.0	**LOUGHBOROUGH.**	

NOTES,

(a) After Six Hills junction, there is an optional but recommended extension of the ride to OLD DALBY, in a beautiful situation in a fold of the Wolds near to the Nottinghamshire border, (See map) Distance 6 miles return.

(b) For alternative route back to LOUGHBOROUGH; From Ratcliffe-on-the-Wreake, after passing under bridge (Fosse Way); cont str ahead (B674) to SILEBY: turn R past church on B5328 to BARROW-on-SOAR; cross River Soar and at TR, cross new bypass then join up with main route into LOUGHBOROUGH. Distance approx. the same.

The banks were covered in flowers as these cyclists climbed through the village of Eaton near Belvoir. Ride No. 9.

51

YOUTH HOSTEL PROFILES.

COPT OAK.

Regrettably, Copt Oak is now the only youth hostel in Leicestershire. (Wymeswold, Whissendine and Bardon Hill, still marked on some old maps, have long since closed). It is popular with cyclists as it makes an ideal base for exploring the north west of the county especially Charnwood Forest.

It is a simple grade hostel and has not changed noticeably since my first visit in 1963. Like many other simple grade hostels, the building was formerly school house. What was once the 'hall' of the school is now a combined common room, dining area and members kitchen but even though it is 'spartan', it is cosy.

Usual hostel meals are not supplied but with reasonable notice, the warden can supply hot snacks. There is a small but adequate store with an emphasis on wholemeal bread and vegetarian food.

Copt Oak is only open on Friday and Saturday nights in the winter when special activities are arranged, many of them specially directed at cyclists. The cycle store is a shed at the rear of the hostel.

THURLBY.

The only other youth hostel near to Leicestershire is Thurlby, a few miles over the Lincolnshire border and 45 miles from Copt Oak. It is conveniently located for the east side of Leicestershire, especially for the Rutland Water area. The hostel is very popular with cyclists and is used regularly by tourists following a cross-country route from Copt Oak to East Anglia.

The attractive house was the private residence of a YHA member who donated it to the YHA as a bequest. It opened as a hostel in 1980. Although there were some internal alterations made, externally the house still looks like a private residence. It has accommodation for 24 with a further 10 in an annexe. It stands in a pleasant situation in the centre of the quiet village in the midst of undulating rural countryside.

Like Copt Oak, Thurley is a self-catering hostel but members have the use of a very adequate kitchen.

The small Youth Hostel at Copt Oak is well placed for exploring Charnwood Forest.

Hallaton has some thatched cottages and an unusual cross. Ride No. 5.

CYCLING GUIDES by ARNOLD ROBINSON.

All contain Route Itineraries, Route Maps, details of Gradients and Surfaces, Touring Information, Points of Interest, Viewpoints and Scenic Attractions, Location of accommodation, Youth Hostels, camp sites, places to eat and cycle repairers. The suggested cycling routes may be ridden as 'day rides' or linked together to form an on-going tour.

Published by The Riding Press, 62 Sheldon Road, Sheffield, S. Yorks. S7 1GX
Cycling around South Yorkshire.

Available from -
Walk & Write Ltd., **Unit 1, Molyneux Business Park, Whitworth Road, Darley Dale, Matlock, Derbyshire. DE4 2HJ**

CYCLING Around CASTLETON and the Hope Valley.
CYCLING Around MATLOCK.
CYCLING Around BUXTON
CYCLING Around CHESTERFIELD.
CYCLING Around LEICESTERSHIRE & RUTLAND
CYCLING Around LINCOLNSHIRE.
CYCLING Around NORTHUMBERLAND
CYCLING Around THE LAKE DISTRICT.
CYCLING Around the NORTH YORKSHIRE MOORS - ten routes which provide an on-going tour.
CYCLING Around STAFFORDSHIRE
CYCLING Around the COTSWOLDS
CYCLING Around the YORKSHIRE WOLDS.
CYCLING Around DERBY
CYCLING Around THE ISLE OF MAN
CYCLING around the PEAK DISTRICT - contains eleven routes which may be ridden individually or linked together to form an 'on-going' tour. Details are also given of the popular off-highway Trails.
CYCLING around SHEFFIELD - nine routes in Sheffield's 'Golden Frame.'
CYCLING around HARTINGTON -touring information and route itineraries.
CYCLING around BAKEWELL - touring information and route itineraries.
CYCLING around ASHBOURNE - touring information and route itineraries.
CYCLING in DERBYSHIRE - eleven of the best cycling routes, mainly in the southern half of the country.
CYCLING in NOTTINGHAMSHIRE - twelve cycling routes which cover most of the county.
CYCLING in the YORKSHIRE DALES, twelve routes which provide an on-going tour
CYCLING around CHESHIRE - twelve routes.

OTHER CYCLING BOOKS from Walk & Write Ltd.,

PEAK DISTRICT CYCLING - Vol 1 - *Round the bend with Graham* - by Graham Kirkby.
PEAK DISTRICT CYCLING - Vol 2 - *Round the bend with Graham* - by Graham Kirkby.

OTHER JOHN MERRILL WALK BOOKS

CIRCULAR WALK GUIDES -
SHORT CIRCULAR WALKS IN THE PEAK DISTRICT - Vol. 1,2 and 3
CIRCULAR WALKS IN WESTERN PEAKLAND
SHORT CIRCULAR WALKS IN THE STAFFORDSHIRE MOORLANDS
SHORT CIRCULAR WALKS - TOWNS & VILLAGES OF THE PEAK DISTRICT
SHORT CIRCULAR WALKS AROUND MATLOCK
SHORT CIRCULAR WALKS IN "PEAK PRACTICE COUNTRY."
SHORT CIRCULAR WALKS IN THE DUKERIES
SHORT CIRCULAR WALKS IN SOUTH YORKSHIRE
SHORT CIRCULAR WALKS IN SOUTH DERBYSHIRE
SHORT CIRCULAR WALKS AROUND BUXTON
SHORT CIRCULAR WALKS AROUND WIRKSWORTH
SHORT CIRCULAR WALKS IN THE HOPE VALLEY
40 SHORT CIRCULAR WALKS IN THE PEAK DISTRICT
CIRCULAR WALKS ON KINDER & BLEAKLOW
SHORT CIRCULAR WALKS IN SOUTH NOTTINGHAMSHIRE
SHIRT CIRCULAR WALKS IN CHESHIRE
SHORT CIRCULAR WALKS IN WEST YORKSHIRE
WHITE PEAK DISTRICT AIRCRAFT WRECKS
CIRCULAR WALKS IN THE DERBYSHIRE DALES
SHORT CIRCULAR WALKS FROM BAKEWELL
SHORT CIRCULAR WALKS IN LATHKILL DALE
CIRCULAR WALKS IN THE WHITE PEAK
SHORT CIRCULAR WALKS IN EAST DEVON
SHORT CIRCULAR WALKS AROUND HARROGATE
SHORT CIRCULAR WALKS IN CHARNWOOD FOREST
SHORT CIRCULAR WALKS AROUND CHESTERFIELD
SHORT CIRCULAR WALKS IN THE YORKS DALES - Vol 1 - Southern area.
SHORT CIRCULAR WALKS IN THE AMBER VALLEY (Derbyshire)
SHORT CIRCULAR WALKS IN THE LAKE DISTRICT
SHORT CIRCULAR WALKS IN THE NORTH YORKSHIRE MOORS
SHORT CIRCULAR WALKS IN EAST STAFFORDSHIRE
DRIVING TO WALK - 16 Short Circular walks south of London by Dr. Simon Archer Vol 1 and 2
LONG CIRCULAR WALKS IN THE PEAK DISTRICT - Vol.1,2 and 3.
DARK PEAK AIRCRAFT WRECK WALKS
LONG CIRCULAR WALKS IN THE STAFFORDSHIRE MOORLANDS
LONG CIRCULAR WALKS IN CHESHIRE
WALKING THE TISSINGTON TRAIL
WALKING THE HIGH PEAK TRAIL
WALKING THE MONSAL TRAIL & OTHER DERBYSHIRE TRAILS
40 WALKS WITH THE SHERWOOD FORESTER by Doug Harvey
PEAK DISTRICT WALKING - TEN "TEN MILER'S"
CLIMB THE PEAKS OF THE PEAK DISTRICT
PEAK DISTRICT WALK A MONTH Vol One

CANAL WALKS -
VOL 1 - DERBYSHIRE & NOTTINGHAMSHIRE
VOL 2 - CHESHIRE & STAFFORDSHIRE
VOL 3 - STAFFORDSHIRE
VOL 4 - THE CHESHIRE RING
VOL 5 - LINCOLNSHIRE & NOTTINGHAMSHIRE
VOL 6 - SOUTH YORKSHIRE
VOL 7 - THE TRENT & MERSEY CANAL
VOL 8 - WALKING THE DERBY CANAL RING
VOL 9 - WALKING THE LLANGOLLEN CANAL

JOHN MERRILL DAY CHALLENGE WALKS -
WHITE PEAK CHALLENGE WALK
DARK PEAK CHALLENGE WALK
PEAK DISTRICT END TO END WALKS
STAFFORDSHIRE MOORLANDS CHALLENGE WALK
THE LITTLE JOHN CHALLENGE WALK
YORKSHIRE DALES CHALLENGE WALK

NORTH YORKSHIRE MOORS CHALLENGE WALK
LAKELAND CHALLENGE WALK
THE RUTLAND WATER CHALLENGE WALK
MALVERN HILLS CHALLENGE WALK
THE SALTER'S WAY
THE SNOWDON CHALLENGE
CHARNWOOD FOREST CHALLENGE WALK
THREE COUNTIES CHALLENGE WALK (Peak District).
CAL-DER-WENT WALK by Geoffrey Carr,
THE QUANTOCK WAY
BELVOIR WITCHES CHALLENGE WALK
THE CARNEDDAU CHALLENGE WALK
THE SWEET PEA CHALLENGE WALK

INSTRUCTION & RECORD -
HIKE TO BE FIT.....STROLLING WITH JOHN
THE JOHN MERRILL WALK RECORD BOOK
HIKE THE WORLD

MULTIPLE DAY WALKS -
THE RIVERS'S WAY
PEAK DISTRICT: HIGH LEVEL ROUTE
PEAK DISTRICT MARATHONS
THE LIMEY WAY
THE PEAKLAND WAY
COMPO'S WAY by Alan Hiley

COAST WALKS & NATIONAL TRAILS -
ISLE OF WIGHT COAST PATH
PEMBROKESHIRE COAST PATH
THE CLEVELAND WAY
WALKING ANGELSEY'S COASTLINE.

PEAK DISTRICT HISTORICAL GUIDES -
A to Z GUIDE OF THE PEAK DISTRICT
DERBYSHIRE INNS - an A to Z guide
HALLS AND CASTLES OF THE PEAK DISTRICT & DERBYSHIRE
TOURING THE PEAK DISTRICT & DERBYSHIRE BY CAR
DERBYSHIRE FOLKLORE
PUNISHMENT IN DERBYSHIRE
CUSTOMS OF THE PEAK DISTRICT & DERBYSHIRE
WINSTER - a souvenir guide
ARKWRIGHT OF CROMFORD
LEGENDS OF DERBYSHIRE
DERBYSHIRE FACTS & RECORDS
TALES FROM THE MINES by Geoffrey Carr
PEAK DISTRICT PLACE NAMES by Martin Spray

JOHN MERRILL'S MAJOR WALKS -
TURN RIGHT AT LAND'S END
WITH MUSTARD ON MY BACK
TURN RIGHT AT DEATH VALLEY
EMERALD COAST WALK
JOHN MERRILL'S 1999 WALKER'S DIARY

SKETCH BOOKS -
SKETCHES OF THE PEAK DISTRICT

COLOUR BOOK:-
THE PEAK DISTRICT.......something to remember her by.

OVERSEAS GUIDES -
HIKING IN NEW MEXICO - Vol I - The Sandia and Manzano Mountains.
Vol 2 - Hiking "Billy the Kid" Country. Vol 4 - N.W. area - " Hiking Indian Country."
"WALKING IN DRACULA COUNTRY" - Romania.

VISITOR GUIDES - MATLOCK . BAKEWELL . ASHBOURNE.